GW00507369

My first client!

John Moat

John Moat

FIREWATER

&

THE

MIRACULOUS

MANDARIN

Barbara —
With my love &
gratitude for
having worked
with you

Antoinette.

ENITHARMON PRESS 1990

And with much good
wishes, John.

First published in 1990
by the Enitharmon Press
40 Rushes Road
Petersfield
Hampshire GU32 3BW

ISBN 1 870612 70 1 (paper)
ISBN 1 870612 41 8 (cloth)

The Enitharmon Press acknowledges
financial assistance from Southern Arts

Set in 9½pt. Century by Heath Setting, Petersfield
and printed by
Strand Press, Petersfield

For Tom Welch

CONTENTS

'But if the life-mass (the *massa confusa*) is to be transformed a *circumambulatio* is necessary, i.e., exclusive concentration on the centre, the place of creative change. During this process one is 'bitten' by animals; in other words, we have to expose ourselves to the animal impulses of the unconscious without identifying with them and without 'running away'; for flight from the unconscious would defeat the purpose of the whole proceeding. We must hold our ground, which means here that the process initiated by the dreamer's self-observation must be experienced in all its ramifications and then articulated with consciousness to the best of his understanding.'

C. G. JUNG, *Psychology and Alchemy*

INVOCATION

Even to exist is a problem
beyond our immediate problem.

Between us
the furnace;
between our eyes
the still, the alembic.
Where our eyes meet —
the substance.

Always it is the truth
before the final truth.

THE QUESTION

I would seem to be here
But there is still the question
Who am I?
She looks away, quickly
But there is still the question
How come I am here?
She smiles, her smile is vague
But there is still the question
What is this pain?
She frowns, she wants me to say I am sorry
But there is still the question
Why are you broken?
She begins to gloat
But there is still the question
Why can't I help you?
She looks triumphant
But there is still the question
What have I done?
Ah now she turns cold
She has almost made up her mind
I have one more chance
This time I must ask the right question.

SOROR MYSTICA

At the outset
It is a moment too soon
One could not say anything for certain
She has her finger to her lips
The sign of caution

When the work is under way
One cannot risk uttering a word
The least distraction and the moment might be missed
She has her finger to her lips
The sign of concentration

At the conclusion
It is already too late
The moment can never be repeated
She has her finger to her lips
The sign of the secret.

THE PROBLEM

What she denies four times is so
Not this this this or this
Nothing beneath the changeable moon
And the world shall end in ice.

What he states three times is true
This this and this again
Nothing else under the sun
And the world shall end in flame.

The constant sun the changeable moon
The three into four won't go
But the balanced world still lives by hope
It may end in fire and snow.

AN EVENT

To begin with, it is silent,
It could be night, or it could just be dark.
He feels he has arrived in a wilderness.

The earth is no longer safe,
The crust is moving in waves,
Is beginning to crack.

Something is about to happen:
The dark is no longer in doubt,
The dark is a prophecy that is beginning to dawn on itself.

Ah, there she is, the white moon —
The non-light sticking to the black violent sky.
This is the beginning.

The black is ready to burst.
The black wind is coming
Out of the horrible mouth of the moon.

The wind has already reached the earth;
It is somewhere behind, somewhere in the wood.
The earth is prepared to respond with violence.

The wood is being taken over.
Someone back there is trying not to scream.
He can feel that scream in his throat — it sticks like a label.

The wind is leaving the wood.
It is coming, it opens the curtains —
It will obliterate everything in the house.

Wait! Somewhere under his feet is the sound of water —
This must be the stream.
The sound is like going back to before the beginning.

The wind thrashes past him;
The scream thrusts its hands over his ears —
So tight he can no longer hear it.

And he can no longer see the light properly;
It has become a blank face staring over his shoulder
Into the face of the wind.

And the face is becoming black.
It has been impressed by the wind,
Is becoming an angel with a black face.

The angel is trying to fasten its mouth over his mouth,
The black breath — he is being smothered in it.
Any moment now everything will have gone black.

The angel is beginning to smile.
It crams his mouth with its black tongue.
The light is going out.

He thinks he can feel a stabbing pain.
He thinks maybe it's his fear coming to a point.
There! the scream again, screaming out of a nick in his thigh.

And the light is opening between his eyes
And under the bridge there is still the water
And perhaps another sound like the sound of voices.

He opens his eyes.
It is night.
The sky is opening out towards the stars.

The air is still, it is windless.
Something settles on his lips — it is like a label.
It is the name that has always been on the tip of his tongue.

The light continues to open outwards —
Beyond it there is light opening
Like the door at the head of the stairs.

He finds he can see past the light
To the light.
He finds he can see all the way.

CHANGELING

He shivers at the sound of the wind
I hold him

He thinks he's in the hulk of a liner, he thinks there's a storm

This neck round his neck has been drawn too tight
I hold him

He wants none of it

He squeals — he can't take this beating
I hold him

His father might find him, he trembles

He is in danger of coming in two
I hold him

He is possessed

He is giving birth, screaming
I hold him

He has mothered an imp

He has fallen into a deep sleep
I hold him

He is terrified by the baboon's laughter

He shakes, he is afraid of his own strength
I hold him

He wants desperately to stand on his own two feet

He cannot let go
I hold him

He is determined to do himself an injury

Someone has let him loose with a knife
I hold him

None of us is safe — she least of all

He screams — and then he screams
I hold him

He wakes with a start

He has seen me, he is opening his arms
I hold him

I am holding him.

THE WAY THROUGH

The baby won't stop crying. This casts a shadow over
  everything.
The devil would love to stop laughing. The laughter's killing
  him.

The baby is in love with his miserable image of himself.
The devil roars with laughter. No one can hear. It drives him
  crazy.

The baby feels his misery is coming along nicely.
The devil laughs. He can match anything for size.

The baby wants his mummy all to himself.
The devil has had mummy. He stuck a knife in her back.

The baby feels guilty. He enjoys every moment of it.
The devil suspects he's in the clear. The thought makes him
  uneasy.

The baby thinks he should hide in the cupboard.
The devil is with him all the way.

This time the baby won't come out until he's ready.
The devil's not sure he's prepared to wait that long.

The baby thinks he hears his dad coming.
'Cave,' says the devil. 'Here comes God.'

There's wind outside. It cuffs the house.
It cuts clean through the building.

The baby opens his eyes. The room is full of light.
The devil lies on his back on the carpet and roars.

The baby has seen the devil.
The devil has stopped laughing.

The baby smiles. He's had an idea.
The devil feels uncomfortable. But can't see any other
way out.

The baby is getting sleepy.
The devil is appalled. The waters are beginning to break.

The baby is asleep.
The devil is in labour.

OPUS

The *imaginatio*, as the alchemists understand it, is in truth a
key that opens the door to the secret of the *opus*... The place
or medium of realization is neither mind nor matter, but the
intermediate realm of subtle reality which can be adequately
expressed only by symbol. The symbol is neither abstract nor
concrete, neither rational nor irrational, neither real nor
unreal. It is always both.

C. G. Jung, *Psychology and Alchemy*

The house is dark
I am not sure what I am
I'm not sure how this will turn out
Everything is possible

1
A curious wind
Is coming from under the floor
Too hot and too rough
Everything it touches needs to tremble
And quite empty
Like a wind turned inside out
Except for its belly
Which is like a stone
Which is full of fire
Which is full of blue water
Which is full of a filmy shadow
Which has yet to make up its mind

2
The hearth
A blue fourstone
Like the still of a river
If it moved it would be transparent
Frozen it conceals everything

Two firedogs loom like water towers
Two grey giants
Everything is on top of them
They have been given no choice
They have nothing to look forward to

3
The spent ash is beginning to dither
Like a tray of pins tapped with a finger
The wind is milking it
The dead coals begin to glow
Something is wriggling into life
Shakes a whisper of grey moondust from its back
Attacks the air
It has leathery wings
Four fiery heads
The whole thing is coming on heat

4
The water in the glass is innocent
The heat fills it everywhere like pain
It chatters on the hob
The floor of the bowl bubbles
Light from four points
Collides in the centre
A rash of colour
A laser phantom
A transfiguration
That would float straight to the surface
Except it's tied to two repulsive animals
Except it's at the end of its tether

5
The heat is stacked in the chimney
The sleeper's lungs are powdery with soot
He dreams the way a stone dreams
With no movement of the eyes
Something he could never imagine
A trap through the sky

6

The water a cloud
Inert as a junket
But the icy wind
Brings it out in a muck sweat
Curdles it like bad blood
Clots it like milk
The whole pail gone off
The father and mother of a mess
The pit of the stomach
Sweet as a tanner's van
The offal shop
The loom
The solar plexus

7

Ravens wriggling out of the black sea
Croaking off through the smoke
With no hope of land
Until this fluke
This rock, this hillock
This enlargement
This mountain shining like darkened liver
In a drench of sweat —
The real heart of the matter
With a topping of snow

8

The wind has blown up an unaccountable treat
Drawn off a rank of cloud from the gungy sea
Clean electric rain
A power line
Running back down the mountain in a silver stream
Enough to melt the heart

9

In the attic the lovers have woken
They can't think how they come to be here
Where the heart of the fire is everywhere
They can't think how they come to be beautiful
They picture each other across a silver sea
Two dark continents
They can't think how they come to be black

10

The sun loses itself in the moon's shadow
The moon is lost in the shadow of the earth
The earth has sunk without trace under the sea

11

The swan is a white shuttle
The swan breathes through the eyes of the wind
The wind doesn't shadow the sky
Or chalk the sea
The swan may not even be there
So that whatever he comes between
Like the sun and the moon
Or the lovers themselves
Are no longer apart

The swan is the white shuttle
The mirror
In which space conceives
The illusion of space

12

A fiery cool breath
Burns up through the floor of the head
Pale and blue as a cloud
We are prepared to drown in it
No thought rides on the surface
I am dragged under
My eyes are out
This silver sea will run everything together
We are forgetting one another

13
What happened then was like waking
The sea had washed everything away
The substance of this circle is single
Fire
But not fire
But not water
But not gold
But equally not silver
No less hers than his

14
Beyond that only the chill fire
The silence that answers the swan's cry
It is the cry of the phoenix

The house is on fire
I am in smithereens
I am this dust of sparks
Flying like silver birds
Fixed like a gas of golden stars
In the face of this brilliant night

FIREWATER

You are like water
A dew-lake
Or a blue meadow
A mist of blue flax
Cornflowers in a meadow of oats

I have dug a deep well
I have struck shillet
I am on fire
I cannot live with myself

You are a rivulet
A ripple breaking on a dark shoreline

I am like a boy
A prince left behind in the afternoon
I have wandered through the empty rooms
Have found my way into the Queen's apartment
Have discovered her wardrobe
And hide in the dark
Feel the blue silk against my cheek
It is liquid
The cool satin
Purple and deep green
I breathe her scent
And the joy of it is like a pain everywhere
I am coming alive

You are uncommonly patient
Nothing can distract you
Your concentration is complete
When you are perfectly still
Then everything is moving
You are wide open
This pinpoint of light
In you it is everywhere
I see it wherever I look

You are like the sea at first light
A pitcher of white gold
In the V of the valley
You are like the bead of water in the lupin leaf
Or like the whole ocean
You are like a riddle
To which the answer is a riddle
To which you are the answer

What is it of me that moves in you?
I am programmed to burn up
What is it about me you respond to?
You have no idea
You have been taken entirely by surprise
You have given yourself away

When I look at you
I catch my breath
When our eyes meet
I feel I might not breathe ever again

You are like midday
Or else a cloudless evening
A blue sky that is mirroring the sea
That mirrors the sky
When you close your eyes
You become unknown
Like a soul in suspense
In the silence between two breaths
Between two heartbeats
Between mantra and mantra
The fire and the fire

My longing is inexpressible
It is as if I must hold my breath
At the same moment as I breathe your name
As if I were seeing you reflected in my own eyes
As if my excitement were drawing joy
From the pain of our being apart
As if in the green shadow beneath the lime-trees
Were the laughter of full sunlight

Like a waterfall in a wood you radiate cold
Your openness accounts for everything
It is irresistible
Everything is enamoured
Flame is drawn to it
Barely touches the surface with its tongue
And the skin sticks
It might be frozen to steel
The surface burns like ice
The skin of the flame is melted
And the fire has run out

Flame is running like water
It is into everything

It has coloured the water sun-red
The whole pitcher is inflamed
The centre is burned out
I don't think I can go on
I am awash with fire

And the air is fire-water
An eau-de-vie
It is pure spirit
I am frightened to breathe

The heart of the fire is gone out
The walls of the kiln will crumble
Water will be into the gallery
It is finding its level
It is becoming like air
No, on the lips it is like milk
With the flavour of fire
I drink

I heard a sound like a sigh

The ceiling is open
It has become a cloud of blue light
A vapour
A breath of smoke

We can breathe again
We can hold our breath

And the blue light over our bed
And in the evening the scent of lime flowers
And the sound of the fountain
And the green woodpecker on the trunk of the medlar
And when the air moves
The tinkle of a string of shells
And from the shadow beside the bamboos
A single blackbird
His song reduced to light

This moment is here
It is where we touch

And the warm night wind on my cheek
Or your cheek or your hair or your breath

Your eyes have opened my eyes
The light is on fire
It is air it is breath
I breathe your breath
Your breath is like blue milk
It is on fire
Your eyes are awash with light
I can see no end to it
I have no more to say.

GENESIS

God was lost in meditation
His own name was the mantra
There could be no distraction

But then God had another idea
If he chose he could become aware of his own breathing
He took a deep breath — everything came alight
He let the breath go — everything became dark
In their own way the light and the dark were equally good

He took another breath, his second
This time the idea was like a bubble, completely round
Probably it was microscopic, though it seemed enormous
Either way there was nothing one could add
It fitted him completely
God felt excited — this was good

For a moment he thought his third breath had been a mistake
The bubble had burst, the whole thing was getting out of hand
It was like a greenhouse,
It was beginning to run riot
Then God saw that he'd had another idea
Everything had suddenly come into flower
Next moment there were seeds everywhere
Each one complete, each one a little bubble
God saw the joke
He laughed, a good belly-laugh
The joke had been at his expense

The next breath was painful
There was still the bubble
But it was beginning to come in two
He must have had the idea that it should be red
Because the pain — it was enough to break one's heart
But when he breathed out, that was the first sigh of content
He felt at home
What had appeared a bad idea was turning out for the best

God took a fifth breath
It occurred to him maybe he was a monkey
This idea stuck in his gullet
He realized he could as easily choose to be a bird
Or a fish
But no, it was this monkey idea that insisted on taking shape
Now when he breathed, the air whistled down inside him
Where it became water fire stone and blood
It was the source of intense excitement
The possibility of getting on in the world
But also of slipping back into a bubble
Or of escaping into chaos
God had no option but to take another breath

The sixth breath — the light hit him between the eyes
It almost blinded him
It was as if he had held up a mirror to his own light
As if his whole experience had assumed a single form
There was the light and the shadow
There was the bubble
And the garden getting out of hand
And the heart come in two
And everything in the balance of one breath
All this in a single figure
As if his *I am* mantra had been translated into form
Soahum, he heard himself say
And with that the image of the man —
Or was it a woman? —
Began to come apart in the light
*I am **that*** — God repeated the mantra
The figure had almost disappeared
It had been perfect, the image of himself
It had after all been an excellent idea
— ***that** I am*, he concluded

Somehow his own name had acquired a new meaning.

God took one last breath
It was complete
Once again he was lost in meditation
Now there would be no further distraction.

THE MISSING BIT

Adam woke
He'd had a terrible dream
That God didn't love him any more
That God had simply torn him in two —
And left him feeling inadequate

He tried to piece himself together
But always the important bit seemed to be missing
It made him want to howl with frustration —
Until he found what maybe he was looking for
Small
Rubbery
Without much shape to it —
But difficult to see a way it would fit

He tried it every conceivable way
Then he had a brilliant idea
He stuck the bit in his mouth
"Mumma" he said with his mouth full

For a time he felt full up
Then he realized he'd made a bad mistake
He yanked himself free
He was back where he'd started

He began to examine the bit minutely
It struck him maybe it was perfectly beautiful
Just looking at it was like heaven
He wanted to lose himself in it
But there was a problem — it was untouchable

Adam was beside himself with frustration
Until suddenly he lit on this wicked idea
Just the glimmer
Like after dark — a forbidden quarter
He felt fired by the idea
Here was something that might really take off

There was more to the bit than he could ever have imagined
Or so it seemed for a time
Until he thought he heard someone coming
He lost his nerve
What if he was found out?
Quickly he dug a hole
Shoved the bit underground and stamped the earth back in
 place

He felt good
He felt full of himself
He even felt prepared to forgive God

But then night came round
And he discovered which bit he hadn't managed to bury
It was the wicked idea

He had trouble getting to sleep
The garden was full of whispering
And then he was dreaming
He was having his old nightmare about snakes
He woke back where he'd started
Frightened of the dark
Inadequate
Unable to get himself together

Adam was out of bed
Was hunting around on all fours in the dark
That bit, he couldn't be without it

There, he had found it
But could he be sure?
It seemed changed
In the dark it felt smooth and round
There was no way this was ever going to fit
Suddenly he had an inspiration
He had missed the point entirely
He opened his mouth and swallowed the bit whole

Next thing he realized the moon had risen
The garden was glowing a kind of moony blue
The grass blue and the clover like glow-worms
The night air was a blue syrup of stocks and syringa
Around the tobacco flowers in the tubs
There were hundreds of loony moths
Glimmering like lamps on the blink
Shot on the moonlight
Their wings humming — mmmmmmmmmmm

Suddenly there was a hole in the sound
Dark, like the night-print of a foot on the lawn
Then another and another
Approaching along the grass path beside the bamboos

Adam was astounded
God was God, but who on earth could this be
He held his breath
He could hear the wrong side of his eardrums
Soft as a finger placed on his lips
The beat of his heart
The soft soundless approach of the footprints.

The girl — so how does one describe her?
She was unexpected
She was carrying a bouquet of blue Christmas roses
She was in her element
She walked slowly, a procession of one
In the silver grass the trail of her hem was dark
She was wearing a blue wedding-dress

And while Adam watched, too amazed to be shy
And while the night air tingled like cold fire
She came and stood in front of him
She didn't look up right away

Adam had begun to worry
He felt sure God was somewhere at the back of all this
He felt probably there was some catch
He felt worried about his role

He felt he was bound to get everything wrong
He felt for instance he might be falling in love
Or that he was about to come up with some wicked idea
He knew something was going to have to happen

And when she did look up
And when Adam saw the blue of her eyes
He felt he had seen through everything
She was like a mirror mirrored in its own reflection
Mirroring itself back and back into its own blue depths
He knew she had taken his breath away
He knew even before she smiled
That she fitted exactly
That here was the mystery that set the seal on the mystery
And when she smiled it was like being given his breath back
And when a moment later their lips touched
The darkness seemed to heal over the two of them
The darkness inside became the darkness outside
He had been turned inside out again
He closed his eyes

It was the estuary, a summer night
The still moment, the night-change of the tide
And then the oak trees on the bank shift in sleep
Like steady breathing
The black starry water is moving back
It is changing everything
The pain of being alone
The indrawn breath of the sigh —
To —
The outbreath
The dark water suddenly free
The tide flooding back into the lungs of the open ocean
All one
All one . . .

Adam had drifted off

The sleep seemed to last for aeons
And the dreams, they were all in the future

He began to feel he was prying on other people's dreams
For instance what was this flood?
And how come he was the sole survivor?
For instance why should he be wrestling with this Angel?
And at the same time be aware of his mistake —
That the angel had been trying merely to embrace him
And then he dreamed he was getting over-excited
And that he might be being tempted to pry on God's dream
And that that could be the most dreadful mistake
But there was nothing he could do to prevent it
Because look, it had already happened
The dimlit stable and the girl in the blue frock
And the mysterious child laughing
And its terrible wound that would never stop bleeding
And this musty earthen smell
Like the smell of gentians
Or of being trapped underground

The dream was coming to an end
The earth was opening
And the light splintering through
Bang between his eyes

Adam wasn't sure whether he was still dreaming
He had a curious heady feeling
He was tempted to believe he was God
He knew then it was imperative that he wake up immediately
Before some darkness happened
Like it was at the outset
He knew he must come down to earth

He woke
Everything was wide awake
He thought he must have just screamed
He remembered nothing
But felt he must have had that same wicked dream
He felt the same pain
He felt certain that this time God really had ripped him apart
So he screamed again
And opened his eyes

Eve was looking at him
She was sitting up beside him in the bed
And was looking at him and laughing
And then she looked at him
For one almighty moment
They knew everything
It was as if they had known each other in a previous life
There must have been some evening in the garden
The cool of the day
And the sound of the fountain
Or as if they had slept together
And everything had been perfect
They laughed because there was nothing to be said
Their only thought was that they shared this one thought
If they were to utter it they would use the same breath
But then it was as if something had distracted them
A word whispered somewhere in the laurels
Or someone moving in the dry brushwood
The other side of the stream
They looked away

When they looked back each saw the shadow in the other's
    eyes
They sensed it was their own fear
They felt they had come apart
They felt they had never taken a good look at each other
In many ways they were completely different
They no longer knew what to think
And down in the clearing there was someone in a foul mood
Yelling, calling them by their separate names
They agreed that at all costs the two of them had to stick
    together
Adam said they must cover themselves
Wasn't this the moment they always ran and tried to hide?
But Eve said No
This time we're going to see the thing through.

MOONEY'S SIN

Mooney toeing his lonely line
Encounters three colourful men
Each one humping a travelling pack,
Mooney a ball-point men.

Those three have their heads in the air
Keeping tabs on a tell-tale star;
Mooney is dazed by the sky herself —
Revealing, blue, demure.

Those three are drawn by Herod the king —
He rules them out of court;
While Mooney recites his twice times two
The others wonder what you do
When 'Shalt not' collides with 'Ought'.

Flush out of ideas beside the sea
The three try to snatch some sleep,
But Mooney retrieves their headlong star
From the blue skirt of the deep.

A stable on the edge of town,
This child with a gleaming grin —
While the three wise men unpack their bags
Mooney commits his sin.

While the three wise men uncover their store
Mooney's heart has sung to a stop —
The child is fine but, heavens above,
This girl with a gift of a lap!

The first unwraps his bar of gold —
The child puts the crown on his head;
Mooney finds he's lost for words,
Smiles at the lady instead.

The second makes much of his pungent stuff
That fills the air like pot-pourri;
Mooney sniffs the cornflower scent
Of this girl the others don't see.

The third has come up with a dreadful thing —
It smells like birth, or the grave;
Mooney lost in her wonderful smile
Has forgotten how to behave.

Round he turns on the three wise men.
Then horror! He's down on his knee —
Father, Holy Ghost and Son,
The awful Trinity!

'Father, Holy Ghost and Son
Your gifts to your smiling boy!
But the awkward gift of my little song
Belongs to the Mother of Joy.

Blue, blue heaven that carries the sun
Withdrawn in the blue above,
Or blue under blue, the reflective deep,
Womb to the stars of dreaming sleep,
Mia Donna and Mother of Love.'

ISIS AND THE ANGEL

An angel in the small hour
Needle-eye and thread
The sky of his secret darkened
By a sandstorm of need

I had asked the question
The appointment was made
But the answer dimmed from his starbrow
To the thought of me in bed

'I never turned on to the winding sheet
To the lethal dose' I said
'Roman candle, golden rain
Leaving me for dead

'The child I get I'll get alone
Needle-eye and thread
A firework that doesn't fall back to earth
A boy with a falcon head

'Lay me open, allow you home —
The word would plummet like lead
The bird we flushed would bolt to earth
In the fire the fire go dead

'All I want is your secret
Needle-eye and thread
The preparation of silver and gold
The way the living are made'

The angel said this power
Was way above his head
But a brighter spark than he'd ever be
Would come back next day instead

An angel in the next small hour
Glows infernal red
His secret shines like an amethyst eye
In a sandstorm of need

His crown a kind of translucent ball
His tongue a brilliant blade
Yet just the one thought — so help me God
To get me into bed

'If I gave in, allowed you where
An angel should fear to tread
Our monoplane would be bound to crash
In the fire the fire go dead

'I want your secret
The recipe for bread
The preparation of silver and gold
The way the living are made'

He glared at me his frosty charm
An ice-age of frozen dread
I stared back the frigid charm
He never got near the bed

He glared and glared a torrid spell
A moment come to a head
I returned the torrid spell
He never got near the bed

At last he lit up — a single flash
Needle-eye and thread
I felt the fire run up the stairs
And geyser in my head

That same moment the universe
Shrugged off its clinker lid
In the fiery oven cooked to a turn
A knob of wholemeal bread

The angel sighed 'So now we know
Don't breathe a word' he said
'Except to the child you've just conceived
The boy with the falcon head'.

MILAREPA AND THE FIVE WISDOMS

To Chögyam Trungpa Rinpoche

VAJRA

His anger mounts
The snow has become a fixed glare

When he tries to breathe
A white sheet is drawn over his mouth

The mountains lean on him
The world closes in

His whole territory has shrunk
To the confine of his head

There is no distinction
Between himself and this blind anger

The world has crowded him out
And now everything is a threat

    Milarepa managed a sigh
    Mountain after mountain slipped back

And it was clearly morning
Cold light on the eastern brim

Winter — the ice in needles
Glittering from the roof

The light spreads like clean water
Feeling its way over everything

A mirror in which the eye sees in each detail
The image of itself

And his mind is extended to cover everything
So everything has room to move

And room to breathe
Without crowding Milarepa

RATNA

All in a breath
And this simple achievement takes his breath away

Look at the gold garden — an unbelievable crop
His satisfaction is a positive danger

So crimson ripe it could split like a fruit
And the black pips — they'd then be everywhere

Even the surrounding stone wall is accomplished
Outside is a world apart

Nothing more to be done — the bees are bored
The ripest pear going soft from the centre

He has completed the house — and the garden
Milarepa realizes with a sense of failure

Milarepa gave up on the riddle — he had seen the answer
That the answer could never come up with the answer

So the thought of being breathless — he shrugged it off
His lungs were full of air

The tip of his finger on the amber earth
He found he had drawn a perfect circle

He let go of the need to let go
Sunlight was already filling his head

He pictured the wall fallen — a grey rubble
Riddled with peacocks and red admirals

When he smiled the intruders walked away
As if he had ceased to exist

Standing in the completed porch he thought
This might be the perfect place to build my house

PADMA

A foxy scent has rushed him off his feet
He's flush with it

Yes this is him — this syrupy oblivion
All he now needs is to be out of his mind

Past that painted face
Painted on the face of his panic

There's room for nobody else
Not if one's to lose oneself completely

If only it were possible to have had her already
Right down to the quick blackout

The business over and done with
Swallowed whole — beginning with his tongue

It happened — in his mind everything was wiped out
Milarepa found himself with breathing space

His breath was so slow he might have forgotten
And she was what was left of the sun — a warm stain

His breathing imperceptible
But the milky flavour gave her away — she was the breath

He thought himself wide open — his lungs were alight
And she overbrimmed she was the scent of bluebells

Another breath
And she showed up in the flowering oak

The open upland settled to the spring night
He stopped breathing — his lungs continued to fill

He breathed out slowly — this time she remained
Milarepa abandoned himself

KARMA

A hailstorm
Has everything springing to life

The white earth begins to come apart
Uncovering a brilliant plot

Now the south wind will never let up —
Heat is thrusting the air like a glove

Grass-seed nettles his skin, pollen his eyes
The cuckoo flies cuckooing into his head

And all the time nextdoor is achieving the impossible
Not a weed between the rows

He listens. The plot is thickening
And somewhere under it all lies his original patch

    Milarepa choked — he wiped his eyes
    The garden stretched to infinity

Evening — shadow had stepped out from the shadows
The green earth had grown together

A white moth collided with the wood
The trees woke quivering

Hookweed hooked the horizon
Drew everything closer

He moved — his foot spilled a lily
In all events he was indispensable

So he gave up and closed his eyes
The dark was neat with a thousand fragrances

When the air is perfectly still, he thought
The four winds are all blowing at once

BUDDHA

Milarepa is beginning to see through everything
Now in winter he hoards his boredom indoors

In spring he can glimpse beneath the glamour
When she walks out of the door she leaves him untouched

In summer he barely registers the fever
As he stands to applaud the bare earth

In autumn with so much wine spilt
Even to get drunk is too much trouble

There remains only himself for company
But these two don't get on so well any more

Boredom is to blame
Inactivity itself is wearing thin

    Milarepa yawned
    Until the black behind his eyes began to scramble

He saw the world turn back to front
Boredom was being torn in two

He saw he was about to quit
He would watch himself walk out of the house

And leave nothing behind — except emptiness
Which was already attaching itself to the memory of itself

He despaired. And it was like being struck with a slipper
He opened all his eyes

Emptiness was filling his emptiness to the brim
There was room for everything — for a hundred thousand
   songs

When nothing is left, he thought
The first star brings everything to light

PRIMAL

God looked down on all of it.
He questioned nothing.
'I am that I am,' He said.
This he had already concluded.

Adam's lips moved in time.
He could only ape the sound.
'I am,' he murmured. 'At least that's what I think.'
He was a complete zombie.

Eve matched him word for word.
'So am I,' she insisted.
Then she put it another way:
'Me too, me too.'

Under his tree, in the shadow,
The snake watched everything.
He smiled. His smile was ambiguous.
'What will be,' said the smile.

LIFE STORY

My father died and left
My mother all to me;
I took her at face value
And that left father free.

Under her loving gaze
I bore my father's stamp
A thing she thought she'd have —
I fixed her in the grave.

So mother's off back to dad,
A manly give and take,
Till being both dead and gone
They both climb on my back.

So then I dug them up
And patched their eyes with stars.
I've packed them off to bed —
While I grow up instead.

SONG

A heartbreak song the life in my vein
A baby locked in stone
But I will steal in the deepest mine
Rubies from the moon

But I will steal in the deepest mine
Rubies locked in stone
A heartbreak song the life in my vein
A baby from the moon

THE SEVENTH WAVE

The first wave broke
Midnight turned over
The curtains moved

The second time
Under the hawthorn
A blackbird sang

Third, a mistake
A single white rose
Her scent missing

Broken in two
The heart is mirrored —
Forms the fourth piece

The fifth last pain
There on your clean sheet
Blood — and water

Her dark sixth sense
A sudden fragrance
Of black jasmin

The seventh wave
All seven flavours
Of the apple.

THREE PROMISES

Between the sheets of midnight and morning
A dream

At first light there's frost
Fields of white manna

In sunlight moment by moment
The day stretches out

A dream, manna, this moment
Three promises you'll never keep.

ADAM AND THE MIRACULOUS MANDARIN

'Oh God,' Adam thought, 'if only — '

He was cut off in mid-sentence
When had God ever liked him getting ideas?

But this time something unusual happened
For one eerie moment he felt he could be in control
That maybe he'd given God the slip
Because this wasn't just some bright idea
This was more like knowledge
Suddenly he knew what he'd always been about to think
That life is like having mislaid something important
That life is this sense of loss
That stuck on one's own there's no point to any of it
God had said, 'You're the image of me —
So get yourself properly kitted out
Take a pride in yourself.'
God might manage to take a pride in *him*self
But for Adam it was existentially a non-starter
Taking a pride in oneself predicated somebody else
Not God
There was no way of impressing God
Because everything God did was by his own definition perfect
No it would need to be somebody else
Somebody different in almost every respect
But at the same time someone on one's beam
Someone who knew how to say, 'That's nice'
Or 'Thank you' or —
Adam was getting worked up —
Or someone who would say 'Yes Adam yes I will I do I love
    you'

There — it had happened again
Definitely uncanny
More of a *déjà vu* experience
Like suddenly hearing something
And knowing it's what one's been listening to all along
Like this queer sound coming from beyond the ceiling

As if there were a room upstairs
And somebody moving about
Shifting the furniture —

Adam held his head in both hands
His imagination had begun to run wild

So maybe there was another room
And maybe the furniture was different
And maybe another room
And a corridor
And a staircase with a stair-carpet
And a pine bannister
And then a landing
And this other room
With blue periwinkles in a vase on the dressing-table
And the door of the wardrobe open
And a pair of little white shoes
With a button and high heels
And laid out on the double bed
This blue dressing-gown

Adam needed to sit down
He felt distinctly odd
He felt electric — as if he'd been turned on
Warm in the middle
And down below he felt — at a loose end
So after all life was full of possibilities
But at the same time there was the spooky feeling
God must have a hand in this somewhere
He'd always fixed everything
Perfectly
Adam began to feel depressed again

Until suddenly he'd snapped out of it
He was looking around him in amazement
Hadn't he been able to conceive of somebody else?
Well didn't that make a whole world of difference?
Not just a variety of possibilities
But infinite choice

Immediately the world appeared in a different light
Everything took on a particular quality
The curtains for instance
Adam had always assumed that curtains were curtains
Synthetic velvet in faded canary yellow
Now he was wondering — was canary yellow quite him
Or these reproductions on the wall — all of them abstract
Or the brass light fittings
Or the G-plan sofa
Or this 12″ plastic and chrome
Japanese Television?

And that's when it began really to happen

Adam had no sooner begun to discriminate
No sooner had his discriminating eye lit on the box
Than a flash of lightning took his mind apart
And there in the centre like a plum on a cracked plate
Was his first memory
God
God laying down the law
God very much the father
Pointing out everything he'd done for the lad
Mains electric fitted carpets you name it
All on an open-ended lease
The rent a mere tithe the small print kept to a minimum
In fact just the single clause
That he Adam
Should never in any circumstances be tempted ever
To turn on
The television

And memory was only the beginning
What was he now coming up with if not the first educated
    guess?
That memory wasn't about to make life any easier
For instance he might be tempted to start living in the past
And if that happened —

Adam was so frightened by the clap of thunder
He never noticed his error
Didn't realize he'd begun to reason with himself
Couldn't think why God should be so mad
Or why he had this creepy idea someone was watching him
Or why he should feel so guilty
Because that's what he did feel — guilty
Guiltily he looked round
And there winking at him
From the shadows behind the television screen
Was this inconceivable creature
It was a — no other word for it — snake
Adam thought his mind was playing him tricks
Something devilish cunning was going on
Like a form of subliminal advertising
He felt he was being got at
But at the same time intensely curious

Curiosity
He remembered about curiosity
That was something that could land him in hot water
It was time to switch off
He tried but it wasn't so easy
He found everything out of control
Thoughts going round and round in his head
He strove to make his mind a blank
Thought he'd succeeded
Was congratulating himself
And then saw that the blank he had in mind
Was the blank television screen
And there was that snake
Grinning from ear to ear
The snake fixed Adam with an ambiguous expression
Adam was fascinated
His mind had become very still
Very clear
Clear and still and cunning — just like the snake's eyes
Suddenly he too began to grin
Adam had twigged
So this was what God had kept hidden in the box

This was God's little secret
Adam was on his feet
There on the side of the box was a button
Marked POWER
And before he could think
And quite oblivious to the cry from upstairs
Like someone in the bedroom having a nightmare
He pushed it

For a moment nothing
Then Adam leapt back
His hands over his ears
From inside the box
Came this uncoiling sound
And then a triumphant hiss
And a moment later the entire screen
Sparkled into life

Adam watched in disbelief

Deep in the jungle
Wading through a green swamp
Carrying above their heads their Kalashnikov rifles
A platoon of black men

Adam felt he'd been ambushed
All in a flash he understood everything
He was able to see what God had in mind
He was catching up with God's latest thinking
He was watching the 9 o'clock news

And then these other buttons
He felt the need to know everything
Every channel the entire programme
Everything that was on God's mind

The top button flip Adam could hardly believe it Coronation
Street flip Come Dancing flip snooker wonderful however did
God come up with these ideas flip the weather forecast flip
Tomorrow's World so God did have it all mapped out flip

Sunday Half-hour flip Adam was on the edge of his seat he'd
not realized everything was so in the balance that the Daleks
might take over the universe it was all up to Dr Who God was
a sick man and so to the last button the one at the bottom
the one marked VIDEO flip —

Adam was back in the jungle
The same green light
And this feverish music
He felt he'd walked in on the middle of something
That what was going on was taboo
Something he wasn't prepared for
That could easily get out of hand
Perhaps what God hadn't wanted him to see

He ran to the set and pushed another button
Nothing happened
Another button
Nothing
The POWER switch
Nothing
Now for certain God would be on to him

But this was compulsive viewing
The green light spilling from the screen
In the music the plot beginning to thicken
And Adam being drawn in
By a string attached to the knot in his stomach
If there was a future to any of this
He wasn't sure he wanted to know

Something's on its way up the stairs
Which is why the three bogeymen run for cover
And why the girl in the window
In the black beret
And little black skirt
The sheeny black stockings
The flame satin blouse
That shows almost everything
Is white as a sheet

Adam felt he'd been held up by a memory
For instance this — no other word for it — girl
She was familiar as the night before
Like the one thing he'd always been alive to
And she wore this wonderful scent
Why he could even put a name to it
Je Reviens and *Ma Griffe*

Enters an old man
A nob down on his luck
Out on his uppers
His tweeds in tatters
He's come in skipping
Following his nose
Has almost caught up with her
Before the trio can catch him
When they find him skint
He's made to pay for it

Or later the one on tiptoe
Hesitating on the stairs
The boy in the doorway
The perfect little angel
She's taken him by the hand
Leads him a slow dance
Shows him the first steps
How a man would hold her
While the three wait in the shadows
Seem to enjoy themselves
But look — the girl's coming alive
She holds the boy closer
Has this look in her eyes
That's too much for the gang
They snatch the pair apart
Do the lad over
Rifle his pockets
Fling him out on his ear

But now they've baited the trap again
The girl back in the window

She appears to have melted
Has discovered what the boy discovered
How a girl loves to dance
So when she looks in the street
She's almost contented
Her lips move as she whispers
But can't catch the name
That's when the storm breaks
The stomp on the stairs
The mackerel take fright — fair-weather fish
The girl's backed against the wall
The door is slapped open

And enters an oddity
He's a man on fire
Or rather in flames
A whirlwind with eyes
Running like the clappers
Seems to know what he's after
Veers like a windspout
A blue upright of water
A hank with sinews like sparkling wires
His hurry is horrible
He runs like a lighted fuse
Makes no secret of his need
In fact he's prepared to bare it
At the same time he does have style
Quite the big spender
Happy to splash the entire lot
Everything on his glamour girl
Before he gives out

No wonder the girl is frightened
She could blow on this voltage
The weight of him — the flash of his colours
Once out in the current
There'd be nothing to cling to

That's when the music slows to a waltz tune
Now you can see her fear is all a front

What's behind is the dream the boy discovered
She steps into it neatly and picks up the time
She holds this one at arm's length
Keeps discreet distance
Her eyes are wide open
What she sees in him God alone knows
She's a wind to his rickfire
He crackles into life
Till in the teeth of the gale
Her hair burns like chaff
He's unleashed she cuts loose
Yet all the time she manages
To hold something back
This drives him crazy
He wants everything at once
So the girl with the weirdest look
As if she's seen the way through
Simply floats like it's happened
Folds in a free fall
He can pick up the pieces
If he choose he will catch her

The three horrormen have their breath back
They share the one shadow
They never guessed what she would sink to
They whisper 'What a miss
The way she enjoys it — there should be a law
And with something that's yellow
That's not even shy to flash it about
He has to be stinking
He's foul with the stuff
No doubt he'll choose to pay on the nail'

The trio then grab him
They're slick as a razor
Quick as a flash
One two then a third
Right to the hilt

They take a step back to admire their handiwork
But now the shock — it's they who've been clobbered
'He's a queer one this the way he keeps flapping
Like the Easter meal after the chop
Cut to the bone still he's on with the jig
He's one track he's cunt-struck he's a chow-dog on heat
But what's odd is he's empty he's come ready-kosher
Three cuts like his cake-hole why can't he dribble
Not a drop of blood in him he's dry as the sabbath'

This time they'll do the job clean
Isn't he the great dangler?
Then belt him to the ceiling
If he's so eager let him hang there
He can watch himself tap-dance
With both feet off the floor
There he's nicely trussed
He won't get off the hook

Adam felt desperate
He felt bound up in this monster
He felt he'd become attached to him
He knew everything was in the balance
He realized that everything now depended on the girl

Something in her's gone soft
She breathes like an apple
Doesn't notice they've dished him
She checks on her hem
And fingers her button
Whatever it was
It seems she's forgotten
Behind her closed eyes
She could still be dancing

The three have their hand-out
Now they've set themselves up
She can do as she fancies
They've provided well for her

They've left him provided for
Quits — time to scarper
In fact they're so eager
The lamp gets knocked over

Now everyone's in the dark

Wait this is eerie
It's beginning to glow
There where it swings
From the hook on the ceiling
Like water impaled
A sack of what's past it
The leavings the offal
With a filament of fire
Showing his colours
Like some kind of lizard
Like a shiny chameleon
Shadowing the room
Like a rainbow in a hailstorm
In the heart of the fire
A broken salamander
That twists on a pin

That's where the girl comes into her own
She's glaring like a pit-shaft
Her eyes are black galleries
A stack of white pupils
Each a minute skull
The dark opens through them
Makes light of the shadow
Pain —
She's cornered that market
She's got it sewn up
What she sees is frozen
Nothing escapes her
She's infernally ugly
Life's come to this standstill
Something's going to give

The hit men they've had it
Too frightened to think
Her glance was enough
They've been put in the shade
But she first wants her boyfriend
She'll have him cut loose
Her oven-bag of giblets
Her light-show of tendons
This luminous ordure
As it slumps on the floor
Why would she want it
The pale shadow of himself?

Adam felt how the music had begun to tingle
He felt he was in a storm of static
That his body was terminal with live cells
And that trapped in each one was the girl's face
The current was making his teeth chatter
He'd begun to shake like a leaf

Her gigolo's reduced to pulp — which is starting to quiver
On the skin-film the lard begins to pump for dear life
She's happy to handle him even when he's injured
Holds him on end like a sparkler that's been lit
He's the spoke on its spindle and she's his wild spinner
Who would have guessed they would want to get spliced
They glide to each other and invent a weird waltz
They clinch in a flash in a shimmy of colour
Spoon and canoodle where they've nothing in common
When he jitters she jives just watch them olé
He's such a bright spark no wonder she responds
Samba bolero la raspa fandango —
When suddenly with one cry the cakewalk is over

They shudder to a halt
The light starts to go
The girl's dance is finished
She's nothing left
She's a jelly
She's gone at the knees

Her breath is like incense — all that's left of the office
She clings to her boyfriend and bites her lip and sighs
But he's shot the spark's gone — too late now for the bellows
In the last of the strange light he's finally busted

Wait what's the glow like a mercury arc-lamp
The place coming alight like the night of merry dancers
He's folded she holds him they're together not there
No wait he's found the spunk to try one more time
He needs the kiss — nothing else will ever content him
Does he make it? I think so but it's hard to be sure
With the light so brilliant it's practically blinding
Wait no wait wait who would believe it?
How could this vestige little more than a vapour
This love stain on the linen like a holy shroud
Unwind in her arms and smile like a baby
While his three crowning wounds have started to bleed?

Adam looked around him at the clear light
It was like coming back to himself in the dentist's chair
Everything in the room staring
In a state of shock
And him not in on the secret
He felt weak as a kitten
That he'd undergone a major operation
That it had taken a lot out of him
There was a pain in his side
And this insistent sickening noise
He felt he'd been aware of it all along
Like a wind in the tree spelling trouble
He must have dropped off
Had probably needed the sleep
He felt he'd been living through a turbid time
That he'd managed to get himself inextricably involved
That he hadn't come through entirely unscathed

And then the noise stopped

The silence — it was clear as the light
Adam began to laugh

The laughter was like letting go
It was like drinking
It was like being born in another dimension —
Fancy thinking it had been the wind
Know what that noise was? It was the hoover
Eve upstairs fixing the bedroom
She'd been up there for ever
Listening to the silence it was as if he could see her
One hand in her hair
She listening and he listening
The pair of them listening
And then he heard what they were listening for
One of the babies had begun to cry
'Adam'
Adam knew better than to answer
'Adam the two of them's woke up
They're starving they're needing their change
It's your turn'
Adam was on his feet
'I'm tied up' he shouted
'Oh God' he heard Eve groan 'Why's it all so boring?'
After a moment she shouted 'Have a look what's on telly'
Adam clapped his hands over his ears
He stood there and waited for something to fall
Nothing happened
Adam began to grin
'Don't ever say it wasn't your idea' he called
And went and pushed the button

For a moment nothing

Then the uncoiling sound
Then the triumphant hiss
And then the entire screen
Sparkled into life.

SONG BEFORE BIRTH

What should I see the house go broke
You swallow it down you swallow it down

What if a shadow as big as a room
You open your arms you gather it home

What should I hear my mother's scream
Open your ears open your eyes

What if a girl and her dress in flame
You open your arms you gather her in

What should you hear her scream again
Open your eyes take a deep breath

What if a dog a wolf or a tiger
Open your throat loosen his collar

What should the idiot jump on my back
Carry him home open your door

What if he stow his boot on my neck
Undo the laces wipe his feet

What should a girl and her dress be red
Open your heart take the knife

What if I see my father come
You gather him in you swallow him down

What should a girl and her dress be green
Take a deep breath swallow the rain

What if the lightning what if thunder
Open your eyes your heart your mind

What should a girl and her dress be blue
Give yourself up drink her down

What if a girl and her dress is snow
Drink her down swallow her breath

What should a girl and her dress be black
Roll up the sky uncover the night

What if her eyes be blank as skulls
Open your arms gather her home

What should I darken the face of God
Unlock your skull let him in

What if the sea the sun or stars
Swallow it down swallow it down

What should I see the world go broke
Swallow it down you swallow it down

And what if that horror that feeds on horror
Breathe on the glass wipe the mirror

NOTES   Page 25   FIREWATER

From a notebook: At first light, in that state between sleeping and waking which seems able to draw on the senses of both, I found myself wondering about the Trinity and the gender of God. My wife was asleep beside me, and I had my hand resting on the back of her head. Suddenly I could feel she was dreaming. A moment later she opened her eyes, looked at me and said in a voice recalled from her dream, "With special emphasis on doing and being being synonymous". I felt immediately, "That's it. Of course."

Page 29   GENESIS

The idea being that The Creation is a drama of self-realization, a *tantric* exercise in which the wakening energy is allowed to mount through the houses of the seven chakras to perfection, or Enlightenment. Or the completion of the Work.

Soahum — 'the supreme mantra of non-duality', a Sanskrit word meaning something like, *I am that* — and so, *I am everything.*

Page 32   THE MISSING BIT

'This Mercurius is composed of body, spirit, and soul, and has assumed the nature and quality of all the elements. Wherefore they affirmed with most powerful genius and understanding that their stone was a living thing, which they also called their Adam, who bore his invisible Eve hidden in his body... ' Dorn, quoted by C. G. Jung in *Psychology And Alchemy.*

Page 38   MOONEY'S SIN

Again it's the problem of the 3 and the 4. Mooney is the imaginative agent that marries the masculine trinity to the feminine quaternity.

The three gifts typify the three persons of the Trinity: Gold, sovereignty; Frankincense, the pervasive fragrance; Myrrh, incarnation and mortality.

Page 43   MILAREPA AND THE FIVE WISDOMS

In his book *Cutting Through Spiritual Materialism*, Chögyam Trungpa writes,'In the Tantric tradition energy is categorized in five basic qualities or *Buddha Families: Vajra, Ratna, Padma, Karma* and *Buddha.* Each Buddha Family has an emotion associated with it which is transmuted into a particular 'wisdom' or aspect of the awakened state of mind. The Buddha Families are also associated with colors, elements, landscapes, directions, seasons, with any aspect of the phenomenal world.'

The associated emotions are as follows, *Vajra*—anger, *Ratna*—pride, *Padma*—passion and possessiveness, *Karma*—envy, *Buddha*—dullness. And these are realized in the awakened state as, respectively, Mirror-like Wisdom, Equanimity, Discriminating Awareness, All-Accomplishing Action and All-Encompassing Space. Thus Buddha can be seen as the 'basic ground', the environment or oxygen that makes it possible for the other principles to function.

Milarepa, poet of *The Hundred Thousand Songs*, became the *Vidyadhara* or 'Holder of the Crazy Wisdom', and as such a personification of Enlightenment through Tantra.

Extracts from the author's essay, *Man's Fall*

I'd bought a record of Bartok's ballet suite, The Miraculous Mandarin. On the cover there was a synopsis of the story. Just the bare details, but they struck with extraordinary force...

Here in brief is the plot: Three thugs in an attic room somewhere in the raw part of town. They have this girl they use as their lure, force her to stand in the window. When the clients arrive up the stairs the thugs do them over, take their cash, and chuck them out. The first to arrive is an old cavalier. The thugs leap on him. He's penniless. They hurl him down the stairs. The second is a boy. The girl comes alive to his innocence, wants him. But he has no money, so the thugs beat him out of the door. They force the girl back in the window. What she lands this time is the weird Mandarin. They hear him coming up the stairs, feel the power of him. He enters like a strike of lightning. He is set on the girl, in a kind of frenzied brutal brilliant need. He's after her. The thugs catch up with him, try every way to do him over, but nothing will bridle his energy, his greed for the girl. They try to smother him. They string him up to the ceiling. They knife him. The fearful wounds mouth, but no blood comes from them. Suddenly the Mandarin begins to glow, a dread *illuminatio*, a green fiery light. The thugs run for it. At last the Mandarin, wounded but his energy intact, catches up with the girl. She accepts him. They dance a wild explorative dance. At last they kiss, long and full. And that does it. The Mandarin collapses. As he dies the blood has begun pumping from his wounds.

A trinity of thugs: a fearful, neurotic patriarchy!

A myth does not, any more than a dream or a poem, have definitive meaning. In fact the contrary — its universal relevance alters in the altered light of particular circumstance. Which means that dream or myth can be endlessly reinterpreted. If, though, this were a man's dream, or Adam's dream, what might he *breathe* from it? That the delinquent male has let his house run dissolute, and keeps the feminine prisoner there, forcing her to work for his material gain. She though is intact — he may whore her, but still she's his living. What he contributes is violence... The old order, the cavalier, is spent, and the new is as yet spunkless, they haven't the lucre. So finally what is this life the feminine is able to raise, this thing that can contain itself no longer? It comes up the stairs and breaks into that room cut off from downstairs, the dingy attic of impaired consciousness. It is the 'alien', the one from the other country. Untameable. And now that he's broken loose in the room he must have the girl. The delinquent male is revolted by him, and scared silly — can't cope with this live thing. But the girl can (remember the unbridled unicorn who lays his unicorn head in the girl's lap?). Their coming to know each other is a demented dance. Finally in the full knowledge of her the Mandarin comes fully alive. His wounds begin to bleed. Yes, he too has learned how to bleed, how to be alive, how to die. At last renewal — rebuilding that house for instance — is possible.

Fear is the negative expression of that male energy whose positive

71

expression is the need, or the desire, to know; the Sun's need to illuminate everything. The negative aspect, fear, is at the back of the thugs' thuggery, at the back of all violence, and the suppression of the feminine. The Mandarin is the repressed positive aspect finally breaking free. He is the ultimately irrepressible need to know. The masculine needs to know the feminine and her embodied knowledge. And the feminine needs to know the masculine because only in her experiencing *his knowing her* is *what she is* made known to her. If an aspect of the feminine (being) is unconscious embodied knowledge, an aspect of the masculine (achieving) is conscious discernment. And what happens when the two do know each other is something else! This is the beginning and the end of the mystery, namely that the fact of their mutual knowing is a separate being. This, in the physical world or the metaphysical, is a child. The child is their knowledge of each other compounded. And its name, among all those other names by which the true alchemist knows it, is love.

The Mandarin, driven by his blind marvellous energy, breaks the hold of the petrified patriarchy and makes it with the girl. In the moment of *conjunctio*, of knowing her, he comes alive to her knowledge. He comes *wholly alive*. His wounds begin to bleed. Secure in her knowledge (the menstrual or lunar knowledge that death is followed by rebirth) he is able to die. And by dying, to come alive. He is thus a contemporary articulation of the alchemical Mercurius — who redeems fallen Adam.